# Creative
# Discussions
# on
# I Corinthians 13

# Creative Discussions on I Corinthians 13

RALPH HEYNEN

**BAKER BOOK HOUSE**
Grand Rapids, Michigan 49506

The material in this book was adapted and enlarged from the Today's Family column of the weekly paper *Bible Studies*, issued by the Education Department of the Christian Reformed Publishing House. We are grateful for permission to use this material in book form.

ISBN: 0-8010-4260-7

Printed in the United States of America

# Contents

# 1

# The Meaning
# of Love

I Corinthians 13 is a song of love. Love is the greatest and most powerful force in our lives. Already as little babies we learn to love mother and father. Soon we extend our love to brothers and sisters, and then to friends and marriage partners. As life moves on, love continues to grow.

In spite of the fact that love is such a basic ingredient in our lives, we use the term *love* very loosely. We say that we *love* pickles or that we *love* cats. We also say that we *love* our parents and that we *love* God. Of course we mean something very different in each case, but we do use the same word.

The Greeks avoided that confusion by using several words for love. *Eros*, first of all, refers to a passionate desire between persons. It is often associated with sexual love and finds its highest expression in the relationship between husbands and wives. The Bible stresses the beauty and importance of *eros* within marriage (Gen. 2:24).

Another Greek word for love is *philos*, the love between neighbors and friends. *Philos* is the base word in *philosophy*, the love of knowledge, and *Philadelphia*, the city of brotherly love. The Bible uses *philos* to describe the love of Jesus for Lazarus (John 11:3, 36) and John (John 20:2).

*Koinonia*, another Greek term, is the love expressed in group fellowship. It suggests a group of people who are studying together or working together at some project of mutual interest. *Koinonia*, then, is the relationship of caring and sharing with one another.

A fourth term, *agape*, is used in I Corinthians 13. *Agape* is love that seeks the highest good, the very best for others. It is a love that demands nothing in return. John used this word when he told us that "God is love." It is the word used when we are told to love God above all and our neighbor as ourselves.

The biblical command is clear: We are to love (*agape*) all kinds of people. Our love has various dimensions and qualities. We love people who are near us or related to us (*koinonia* and *philos*). The full expression of our love as *eros* is reserved for the one we love dearly, our mate. But the highest love, *agape*, the love which describes God and which we are commanded to observe, is a love without prejudice or qualification. It is to extend even to our enemies and to those who, by human standards, are unlovable. While other kinds of love may be affected by time and circumstances, *agape*, the love of which Paul speaks, "bears all things, believes all things, hopes all things, endures all things."

In our study of I Corinthians 13 we must notice another dimension of *agape*. True love does not have its origin in people, but in God. God first loved us, a love made personal in Christ. As the apostle John writes in his first letter: "In this the love of God was made manifest among us, that God sent his only Son into the world, so that we might live through him. In this is love, not that we loved God but that he loved us and sent his Son to be the expiation for our sins. Beloved, if God so loved us, we also ought to love one another" (I John 4:9-11). The love we receive from God must be reflected back to God and to our fellow human beings. As we continue our study of I Corinthians 13 in future weeks, we will see more clearly the aspects of this love. We will emphasize the expression of this love in the home, the place where our earliest training in love takes place.

There is always a price for loving, but there is also great personal satisfaction. Paul encourages the practice of realistic, risk-taking, life-building love. In the Corinthian church there was much strife and conflict. Paul dealt rather firmly with this in his letter. In chapter twelve he talked about the various gifts of the Spirit. The attention some believers gave to these gifts brought strife within the church. At the conclusion of that chapter Paul wrote, "And now I will show you a more excellent way" (I Cor. 12:31). This more excellent way is the pathway of true love. We all need—in an ever larger measure—this greatest gift of the Spirit.

## Discussion Questions

1. This passage implies that true love comes from God and is revealed in Christ. If this is so, how can an atheist or a nonbeliever genuinely love a spouse, children, or neighbors? Are there levels of love?

2. Occasionally every married couple has quarrels and arguments. Does this mean that they do not love each other? How can you explain such conflicts in a loving marriage? Would you enjoy a marriage in which there were no conflicts? Why, or why not?

3. Our age abounds with erotic literature, movies, and lifestyles. How is this a barometer of our times? How should a Christian react to the emphasis of sex on TV?

4. In Matthew 5:43-48 we are told to love not only our neighbors but also our enemies. Is it possible to love our enemies? How can we learn to love those who wrong us or persecute us? Is it possible to love a person even when we do not approve of his lifestyle? Why does Jesus give this command which seems almost impossible to obey?

5. Many Christians seem reluctant to be involved in a group study of the Bible or the Christian life. Is this caused by a lack of *koinonia*? How can *koinonia* be developed in the church today?

6. Love is something that must be cultivated and exercised. What can today's Christian do to reflect love? Do you feel that you have been instrumental in creating a greater spirit of love in your community? How can there be greater love in our highly competitive business and labor world?

7. What are some of the results of conflicts within the church and between denominations? What can we do in today's church life to overcome such clashes?

# 2

## The Language of Love

### I Corinthians 13:1
### James 3:1-12

We all have favorite ways of expressing our love to each other. It may be a sentimental greeting card, a love poem, a note, or a quick "I love you" as we part for the day. Some of us are very profuse in the language we use to express our love, others are more casual.

In this song of love, Paul mentions the "tongues of men and of angels." Some people focus on the "tongues of men" and conclude that this refers to the experience of speaking in tongues. Others focus on the "tongues of . . . angels" and from this comment on the language of heaven. But Paul's emphasis is not on tongues. Paul is telling us that eloquent and lofty words are empty and hollow without love. They are like the clanging sound of brass or the ear-jarring crash of cymbals. Such words never touch the heart.

Language is a precious gift. It breaks the barrier of our loneliness as we reach out to others. It is our primary tool for communicating with each other. Although eloquence is admirable, the real power of language is not in the choice of beautiful

11

words, or in the mellow music of a voice, but in the sensitivity of the person who speaks. If words do not flow from the heart, if they are not accompanied by deeds of love, they are empty and hollow and of little value or beauty. Such words may touch the membrane of the ear, but they never reach the corridor of the heart and soul.·

Possibly this is one of the reasons for our lack of response to the thousands of words that reach our ears each day. The speaker who is not sensitive to the needs and desires of an audience; the pastor who speaks with little evidence of a love for souls; the parent who lectures a youngster without real understanding—all these make empty and discordant noises. This is not the language of love.

The Bible insists on harmony between words and deeds. The grand example of this harmony is in "the Word become flesh" in Christ. The love of God entered into the stream of humanity in the person of Jesus. He came, not just to tell the truth, but to be "the Truth." The same thing must happen in our family life; our words, our vows, and our commitments must be translated into deeds and lives of love.

Much stress is given to communication in the home. Often what we say to our mates, to our parents, and to our children is merely a recital of facts or a series of judgments about things. Such communication is superficial. We must also learn to talk about our feelings and emotions—to honestly open our hearts to others. While this deeper form of communication is not as frequent outside of the family, the home requires it. It is from this source that we express the true language of love.

The mother of Andrew Murray, a pastor who left a large legacy of beautiful devotional material, was asked what she had done to be so successful with her rather large family (five of her sons were in Christian work). She said, "I really didn't do anything. I just lived the way I wanted them to live." The power of example is a force that reaches far deeper than the power of human words, no matter how beautifully they are spoken.

Living the Christian life includes words, songs, and prayers. But these must be given shape in the deeds and actions of day-to-day living. And both words and actions must be consistent with the basic principle of love.

The apostle James teaches us that although speech is a glorious gift, it can also be used in a devastating way. Eloquent words, words of understanding and caring, can help others lift their burdens. But a vile tongue filled with anger, slander or cut-downs can hurt others deeply. Speech depends on what lies in the heart of the one who speaks, for we reveal ourselves in the words of our lips. Our words communicate our inner feelings towards others.

We join in the prayer of the psalmist, "Set a guard over my mouth, O Lord, keep watch over the door of my lips" (Ps. 141:3). We need the help of a loving God to speak the language of love.

**Discussion Questions**

1. Some cultures are open in expressing love, others are less so. To which culture do you be-

long? What influence did your parents have over the way you express love for others?

2. Words of endearment are often used to express love. Is it possible that couples become so accustomed to the use of words like *honey* and *dear* that such words lose their real value? How can they be a cover-up for underlying negative feelings or lack of love?

3. Youngsters and teen-agers often say to their parents, "Don't preach to me." Why is preaching, which we value highly in our churches, often used in such negative ways outside of church? What is sometimes missing in our pulpit preaching?

4. Today people talk a great deal about lack of communication in the home, in business, and in institutions. Do you feel this is due to a lack of talking with each other, or is it caused by words that do not flow from the heart? Is the communication problem due to a lack of love for each other? Explain.

5. Some people, such as factory foremen, office managers, or head nurses, are required to communicate orders and procedures to others. While many can do this effectively without causing resistance, others cannot. What is the difference between one who is effective and one who builds resentment? Can this same principle make one pastor or teacher successful, while another is a failure? How can we develop better communication skills?

6. When some witness of their faith in Christ they antagonize the person they are trying to reach.

14

Is this due to the techniques used, or [?]
titude of the heart? Can we be an effecti[?]
ness if we do not have love for others? [?]
is your reaction to classes in personal witness-
ing? Are they an effective teaching tool?

7. What are some nonverbal ways of communicating love? Do you feel they are as effective
as the spoken word? Why, or why not?

8. In some churches the greeting "God loves you,
and so do I" is used in every service. How do
you react to the use of this phrase in worship?
Do you feel that it is meaningful or meaning-
less? How do you suppose it would affect a
visitor?

# 3

## Knowledge Without Love

### I Corinthians 13:2
### Job 38:1-11

*"If I . . . understand all mysteries and all knowledge . . . but have not love, I am nothing."*

For a society which places a great premium on knowledge and degrees, Paul's words are sometimes difficult. Most of us have great respect for people who have proven their intellect. We honor people who have the knowledge and skill to create an atomic weapon, a polio vaccine, or a sensitive novel. But, says Paul, if they "have not love, [they] are nothing."

Knowledge without love can be easily understood by using the family to illustrate. A sister who uses her education to belittle her siblings and show off her knowledge or a father who always has the "right" answer for everything are but two examples. Such a sister or father drives the rest of the family mad. Why? Because a person's knowledge is of little value if he or she has no concern for other human beings.

This doesn't mean, of course, that knowledge is insignificant; it is a marvelous gift of God. Christians are not like the owl that lives in the dark, but rather like the eagle that soars in the sunlight. We are encouraged to learn. We should spend our lives increasing our knowledge, always remembering that knowledge is subject to the higher law of love.

Our schools do a good job of imparting facts, dates, numbers and theories, but I wonder whether we stress feelings and emotions enough. Many brilliant students still have little to equip them for real living; they have not learned to apply their knowledge to the world in which they live and, especially, to human relationships. A brilliant mind is worth little if the individual is not also mentally healthy and whole.

For this reason the family must play the all-important role of training children in the art of loving and living. Setting the pattern of behavior and the sense of values which will lead into wholesome spiritual and moral living must always be the high calling of parents. They must make a definite effort to teach their children to be warm, accepting, understanding, and loving persons.

Love may solve few problems. It may leave many questions unanswered. It may even cause struggles and perils in life. But it is the only way. God not only understands us; He also loves us. According to Job 38, there is nothing that escapes the knowledge of God. Knowledge and love are blended together in all God does for us and in us. And it is this combination of perfect knowledge and perfect love which must be our ideal and our goal.

Paul's expression is hypothetical: no one has

all knowledge; no one knows all the mysteries of life. But he uses these extremes to stress the supremacy of love. We can have an intellectual knowledge of all the truths and creeds of the Bible, be able to quote large sections of the Bible, or hold our own in an argument about doctrine; but if we lack the one great ingredient of love for God, our family, our neighbors, and ourselves, "we are nothing."

## Discussion Questions

1. When you apply for a job today you are usually required to be a high school graduate. Often a college degree is needed. Do you feel the emphasis on the diploma is necessary? Are there other things that are more important? What are some of these?

2. How do you deal with a person who is a know-it-all? Could it be that a person who feels the need to show his superior intelligence may be insecure? How can we discern between someone who is really insecure and someone who is arrogant?

3. What does Paul mean in I Corinthians 8:1, "Knowledge puffs up, but love edifies"? Does this apply to all knowledge?

4. At a certain stage in development many teenagers feel that they know more than their parents. List some ways of dealing with this condition.

5. Is there a danger of schools putting too much stress on the intellectual side of education at

the expense of emotional and character development? How could the educational system become a better character-building agency?

6. Would it be important for a church considering a new pastor to know a prospective pastor's IQ? A high grade-point average is needed to enroll in medical school. Do you feel this is a good idea? How can a person be brilliant and yet not be a good pastor or doctor?

7. How do you like the remark "My dad (mother) was not well educated, but he was a marvelous father (mother)"? Does this show a good spirit between parent and child?

8. The Bible tells us that God is all-wise and the source of all wisdom. We are also told "God is love" (I John 4:8). What does this tell you in the light of the passage we are studying?

# 4

## Giving—An Act of Love

### I Corinthians 13:3
### II Corinthians 8:1-9

"Not what we give, but what we share,
For the gift without the giver is bare;
Who gives himself with his alms feeds three,
Himself, his hungering neighbor, and Me."

These words of James Russell Lowell in his "Vision of Sir Launfall" express a healthy approach to giving. The lesson the knight in search of the Holy Grail had to learn is the same lesson Paul presents in these passages from First and Second Corinthians.

Unfortunately, much giving in our world is not motivated by love. Many people give to the Cancer Fund, the American Diabetes Association, or the Red Cross not because they love their neighbor, but because they love themselves. Television commercials assure donors that, if they give to these causes, someday when they, or someone they love, need help they will receive it. This type of basically self-centered giving is like an investment. It may be a good investment, but it is not an act of love.

Other motivations for giving are competitiveness and pity. Over the Labor Day weekend Americans can view a telethon designed to raise funds for muscular dystrophy. Many well-known celebrities present their talent and make their plea. A child in a wheelchair is "displayed" to evoke feelings of sympathy or pity in the viewers. Sometimes one town challenges another town to raise more money than they do. The telethon leaders usually gather some thirty million dollars, but often that money is not given out of love. Unfortunately, we frequently resort to the same methods to gather funds for the church or church-related work. One Christian orphanage used a lottery to encourage prospective givers to "take a chance" for the benefit of some poor child.

The one great requirement of true giving is to give out of love—love for God, love for Christ, and love for our neighbors. We have defined love as "the power to respond to the needs of others without expecting rewards." Such giving asks no return on its investment. Instead of bartering in benevolence, we give simply because others have needs. We also give *ourselves*. Ephesians 5:25 tells us that the love of a husband for his wife is self-giving, "even as Christ gave himself for the church."

We often think of giving only in terms of church, charities, and missions. But benevolence and compassion begin at home, and it is to our families that we are first called to give of ourselves. Love for our mates, our children, our parents, and our brothers and sisters is a special kind of love. Such love has a closeness, an immediacy to it, that love for neighbor cannot quite achieve. In an article which appeared in many newspapers, Don Shoemaker referred to children as "High-Priced Bundles of Love." He estimated that it costs about $30,000 to raise a child from the nursery to high school graduation. By today's standards that figure seems low, especially if our children attend a Christian school.

However, because of the special love in a family, we don't count the cost of our children in terms of money. We all realize a great deal of personal sacrifice is invested into each child, but we are usually content to make such sacrifices. We want our children to rise to greater spiritual heights than we ourselves attain. We want them to be morally strong—loving and caring to others. All these things demand personal sacrifices of love. Some of us are quite limited financially while our children are growing up and being educated; we often have to go without some things. But looking back at those years, most of us will feel they were the best years of our lives: there is something rightly rewarding in the self-giving love in the family.

God loves us with an uncalculating love: He did not ask what it would cost to send His Son into the world. He asks the same love from us. We keep on giving because we love our neighbor, we love our mates, we love our children. Paul says that is the way we ought to live.

At the funeral of a ten-year-old boy who had died of a bone disease, the father said tearfully, "It cost us a large sum of money for medical care and expense. We did all we could. Now we don't have to pay for him anymore—but how we wish we could. There is a far greater price we pay for the empty place in our hearts."

## Discussion Questions

1. How do you feel about the money-raising methods used for many good causes? Which methods do you find objectionable? Are these methods used to prompt people to give who would not ordinarily do so? Is there an honest way to get people to give?

2. What is your reaction to the appeals for funds used by TV preachers and evangelists? What do you think of giving trinkets, or literature, as incentives for people to contribute?

3. Is tithing a good method of giving? Does it make giving somewhat mechanical and calculated? Is it giving out of love?

4. Why are we more inclined to give to the Heart Fund when a neighbor comes to our door than if a stranger were to ask for a contribution? Is that giving out of love?

5. How do you react to telephone calls soliciting for funds?

6. We hear a great deal about world hunger and the sin of waste in our own land. Does it help the hungry people of the world if we eat less? What can we do to alleviate a problem of such large dimensions? How do you feel about a day of fasting for world hunger?

7. Is the matter of giving Christmas presents overdone in our land? When Christmas buying gets

24

to be a family burden, are gifts still an expression of love for those who are to receive the gifts? How should we approach giving at Christmas?

8. Your supervisor is leaving. You dislike your supervisor but give money when coworkers come collecting for a farewell gift. How much love is expressed in such giving? Would it be better not to give such gifts?

9. Are contributions to the church given as an act of love or out of a sense of necessity? The pastor speaks of "love offerings." Are they?

# 5

## The Kindness of Love

### I Corinthians 13:4a
### Matthew 18:21-35

Throughout I Corinthians 13 Paul extols the power and beauty of love. Love, says Paul, is greater than the speech of men and angels, greater than knowledge—yes, even greater than personal sacrifice. Like a prism divides light into the various colors of the rainbow, so the unique characteristics of love are presented to us in the next few verses. In our study we will trace these qualities in the various relationships in marriage and the family.

"Love is long-suffering" or, as others translate it, "Love is patient." "Long-suffering" or "patience" is the acceptance of others around us. Our neighbors may be hard to live with; they may be annoying and difficult. Our first reaction is to resent them, to be offended or even angry with them. But this is not the way of love. In love we accept people even though we may not like the way they act or live.

This is also the essence of God's long-suffering attitude towards us. We often wonder why God was patient for such a long time with His rebellious people in the Old Testament. It is sometimes hard for us to believe that God is willing to accept us even though our lives so often show a lack of love and trust for Him. Jesus shows this spirit in the years of work with weak-willed disciples who often disappointed Him. The parable in Matthew 18 shows the contrast between a forgiving God and unforgiving humanity.

In the family we need that same spirit. Husbands and wives are not always lovable. We often treat other family members rather shabbily. The spirit of love enables us to accept others even when they cause us pain. The word *long-suffering* implies that out of love we are willing to suffer and to do so patiently for the benefit of another. Of course, we must not suffer interminably. There are times when we must call a halt to what a mate or child is doing to hurt us. But we must remember, love requires that we suffer longer and more deeply than we, and others about us, think we should. Such patience is not spinelessness; it is love in action.

Paul's next word further defines a patient love: "Love is patient *and* kind." To be only long-suffering can create a vacuum: We can ignore a neighbor until things cool off, but such a retreat does not show love. Kindness is a power that conquers even our enemies (Rom. 12:20-21). To go the second mile, to turn the other cheek, requires a good deal of maturity, a quality developed in response to God's kindness to us.

Can we be too kind, too magnanimous? Kindness to another—a neighbor, a spouse, a child—ceases to be kindness when it does not seek for the real good of another. Kindness can be weakness when it is used unthinkingly. It is weakness, not kindness, which prompts a person to give candy to an angry child just to escape the problem. Kindness must be used with wisdom and discretion. It must be motivated with genuine love which flows from a confident heart.

Kindness and long-suffering play a large role in family living, but we must make sure these are genuinely expressed. The Pharisees showed kindness by their gifts, making a show of giving alms, but their actions were seldom from the heart. The widow's mite was more to Jesus' liking. A kind word or deed can often smooth the ruffled feelings in a family. The little deeds of helpfulness, the word of affirmation, the smile that shows acceptance make family life something beautiful.

The courage to love also helps us to be ourselves and to allow others in the family to be themselves. Practicing patience and kindness involves a risk, the risk of playing a role. But when we see and feel in our hearts the power of God's patience and lovingkindness, we—His image bearers, His own children--will dare to take the risks. We need both to receive kindness and to give kindness to live a full life in the home.

**Discussion Questions**

1. A woman is married to an alcoholic who often abuses her when he is drunk. How long should she patiently endure the situation? Where are the limits to kindness in such circumstances?

2. Children are sometimes smothered with love and overprotected in the family. When is there too much protectiveness and kindness? How can we tell whether we are guilty of this in our families? Do you feel your parents were too protective with you?

3. When we say someone is a kind person, what do we mean? Would you like to have others say this about you? How can we tell whether kindness is genuine?

4. In Galatians 5:22 kindness is listed as one fruit of the Spirit. Does the Spirit of God inspire this quality, or are some people naturally more kind than others? What means does the Spirit use to bring out this quality of the Christian life?

5. If your boss is described as a kind person, many will consider that it is easy to take advantage of him. Can a person be kind and yet firm? In hospitals nurses are instructed to treat some patients with kind firmness. What does this mean?

6. Parents need a great deal of patience in bringing up children. Should we also expect that children learn to be patient with the weaknesses of their parents? How can we teach this?

7. It often takes patience to deal with elderly parents. How patient and kind must we be? When is placing them in a home for the aged, or a nursing home, an act of kindness?

8. A couple lived in four different homes and always seemed to get neighbors that they de-

scribed as being "hard to get along with." What is your view of that couple? Should we be able to get along with neighbors no matter what?

# 6

## Love and Jealousy

I Corinthians 13:4b
Numbers 12

Most of us have, at times, felt the pain of jealousy. It is very common among children who suffer from sibling rivalry. It is common among adults as well.

Some jealousy is wholesome. We read that God is a jealous God, meaning that He desires to be the only object of our worship. There are to be no other gods before Him. Sometimes people are wholesomely jealous too. Paul says of the Corinthian church: "I have been jealous over you with a godly jealousy" (II Cor. 11:2).

God demands our exclusive loyalty because he is sovereign. Such loyalty and wholehearted love is also a worthy trait in marriage. But when this desire leads to an overly possessive type of love it promotes an unwholesome jealousy.

Some translators use the term *envy*. Envy is usually presented as the "green-eyed monster" that leads to many unworthy attitudes and acts. Cain was envious of Abel. In the parable of the prodigal son the elder brother was envious of the attention paid his returning younger brother. Jealousy often rears its ugly head in marriage and the family.

We have noted before the difference between erotic (*eros*) love and the higher type of love (*agape*). In the intimate relationship of marriage we have a right to expect a unique love from our spouse which he or she expresses to no one else. There is an exclusiveness in the sexual area of life. The Bible demands this and has strong words about infidelity. If mates do not trust each other in this area, there is often very unwholesome jealousy.

Paul, in this hymn of love, seeks to describe a love not conditioned by the erotic aspects of life, but a love hallowed by faith in God. Christian love possesses a power to rise above the anxious feelings of envy and jealousy. It has in it the element of trust—a trust conditioned not by human circumstances, but by the faithfulness of God. The perfect love, love begotten in God and shining through us, His children, is a love that is not jealous, a love that is not envious. It does not demand that the other person be so possessed by us that he or she loses the freedom to be a real person. This godly love does not seek to make the one we love merely an appendage of ourselves.

We often observe couples who are like that. A man marries a carefree and capable woman, then tries to rob her of that spirit and make her over into a carbon copy of his own mother. A doctor, or a pastor, attempts to make his wife his assistant even though her talents lie in quite a different field. Some men say, "I don't want my wife to work after we are married," even though she would feel more comfortable and fulfilled in continuing her work. In the same way some wives have tried to make their husbands lovers of symphonic or operatic music—when they would far rather be playing golf or tennis.

Love demands that we respect the object of our love, that we give the other person room to live his or her own life. We must be willing to sacrifice for his or her welfare. The basic goal of every marriage must be one of personal and mutual growth. You cannot have one without the other. There are husbands and wives who feel they have outgrown their mates. One has had the opportunity to grow intellectually, culturally, or professionally, while the other has remained at the same level. This does not give reason for growing apart. It does mean that real love has not been exercised in helping the other to grow.

Love rejoices over the blessings of others. It does not begrudge others for what they have or have become. Petty jealousies may develop in the family when a married brother or sister is more prosperous than the rest. These petty jealousies often rob people of the enjoyment of the blessings they do have. They enjoy their home or car until a brother or sister has something better. Such jealousy has no place in the family. It destroys good relationships and mars the love of which Paul speaks.

Jesus taught a new and positive way of living: "A new commandment I give to you, that you love one another, as I have loved you" (John 13:34).

Such love, demonstrated by Christ and given to us through the Holy Spirit is patient and kind; it is not jealous or boastful.

**Discussion Questions**

1. Paul says that love is not jealous, that God is love, and yet Paul also says that God is a jealous God. How can we understand the jealousy of God?

2. We often envy the person who has more money and possessions or more abilities and talents than we have. How do you deal with feelings of envy and jealousy in your life? How do you handle jealousy in your children? Can a Christian overcome all jealousy? Why, or why not?

3. In the story in Numbers 12, why does God deal so harshly with Miriam? Since Aaron was also guilty, why was he not disciplined?

4. How do you feel about a husband who tries to make his wife into a carbon copy of his mother? How about a wife who tries to make her husband over into her own pattern? Is one of the purposes of marriage to help the mate to develop and grow, or do we accept our mate as he or she is?

5. There is much envy and jealousy among teenagers especially concerning boyfriends and girl friends. How can we teach them the art of love and respect for each other? How did you handle your jealousy feelings when you were a teen? How do you handle jealousy now?

6. In businesses envy often erupts in the form of nit-picking and faultfinding. When fellow workers criticize, how can you tell whether they are merely envious, or whether their criticism is genuine? How well do you accept criticism?

7. Dr. Lewis Smedes in his excellent book, *Love Within Limits*, writes, "Agapic love is the power that diminishes the pain of jealousy, because it keeps us from expecting too much from another finite person." What is your reaction to that comment? Do you think it works? Why, or why not?

# 7

# The Humility of Love

## I Corinthians 13:4
## Luke 18:9-14

Jonathan Edwards, the Puritan preacher, once said: "Nothing sets a person so much out of the devil's reach as humility." An equally true statement might be "Nothing sets a person so much *in* the devil's reach as pride."

Pride is one of the Christian's greatest enemies. We often boast and brag when we don't think well of ourselves. To cover up self-doubt and a poor self-image, we become proud, hoping people will then think well of us. But usually our pride creates bickering and disagreement and leaves a trail of blunders and embarrassments in its wake.

Pride makes people difficult to deal with. They will seldom admit they could possibly be wrong and are easily offended. They often feel others do not understand their true importance. Pride is unyielding, often demanding, never tender or considerate. And pride demands a terrible price: it stands in the way of true love.

We often use the word *proud* rather loosely. We say we are "proud" of our families or our children. We may be "proud" of some special accomplishments and worth of others around us. The difficulty enters when we think we must remind others of our own accomplishments and worth.

Paul tells us love is not boastful—not puffed up. There is nothing wrong with enjoying the praise of others, but when that praise leads us to think we are better than others, pride has entered and stifled love. When we boast, either silently or publicly, we are lacking in one of the qualities of genuine love—humility.

There are various kinds of pride. One is a form of intellectual snobbery. When we hear some people talk, we get the feeling they're talking down to us. They respond like Caiaphas to the Jewish high court: "Ye know nothing at all." It is not so serious when a stranger takes that attitude with us. But in the family such boastfulness can be destructive to relationships.

Another form of pride which afflicts many of us is the pride of possessions. In some areas the quality and size of a house has become a status symbol. Clothing, furniture, swimming pools, and nearly everything we own can make us proud. Recent court cases have publicized the difficulties money and possessions can cause between husbands and wives, especially when the marriage is dissolved.

To teach lessons in humility our Lord presented a number of parables which reveal that pride conflicts with entrance into the kingdom of heaven. He taught His disciples to become like little children—not childish (for pride is a childish trait), but childlike. The proud Pharisee finds little room in the kingdom of Christ.

In recent years much emphasis has been placed on developing a healthy self-image. If we are to love our neighbor as ourselves, we must first love ourselves. This does not mean that we compare ourselves with others, but that we see ourselves as worthwhile creatures of our Father's hand, as persons for whom Christ died. We bow low in the presence of God, but we walk confidently and securely in the presence of others. A person with a good self-image does not have to boast.

True love is directed to things outside of ourselves. We accept who and what we are. We also accept others for who and what they are. Living in love, the love with which God loves us, we can rejoice in who and what we are. We rejoice also in who and what our mate is, or better still, what we together have become through God's grace. A proud person has no room for growth; he or she feels he has arrived. If marriage is to be a growing relationship, as it should be, only the humble can find his or her place there.

There is more pride in most of us than we are willing to admit. To grow in true love we must work at overcoming pride. Together, the family as a unit must strive to build a healthy self-image in each member and, at the same time, to develop the kind of love that conquers boasting and pride.

**Discussion Questions**

1. What is the difference between pride and self-esteem? Should Christians say, "I'm proud of my family" or "I'm proud of my house"? Why, or why not?

2. Why is it difficult to live with a proud husband or wife? What happens when two proud people marry? How should we deal with haughty youngsters in the home?

3. In some countries castes (classes) are clearly defined and distinct from one another. How are class distinctions expressed in the Western world? How does this fit in with the law of humility expressed here?

4. Is it possible to be proud of our humility? What results?

5. Are you proud of your church? Should you be? What qualities in a church give us the feeling of pride? Some churches appeal to wealthy members; others to intellectuals. Is it possible to avoid class distinction in the church? Should we? See James 2:1-8.

6. A widow with several children and a meager income was said to be "too proud to receive charity or welfare." Is that a virtue? Can our pride stand in the way of our personal or family's well-being?

7. Some psychologists tell us that persons who have a proud and boastful appearance are really only covering up their feelings of inferiority and inadequacy. How do you feel about this? If this is true, are there genuinely proud people?

8. Why does the Bible condemn pride? Must we conclude that humility is one of the most important virtues of the Christian life?

# 8

## Love's Courteous
## Behavior

### I Corinthians 13:5
### I Peter 3:8-9

Many of us conduct ourselves courteously for no other reason than that others may think well of us. We give each other the glad hand. We smile a great deal when we exchange greetings. It's good salesmanship for selling ourselves. But often, the relationships that result are very superficial.

When Paul says love is courteous, he has something else in mind. True love is not only an inner attitude; it also reflects itself in the way we live with others. Love calls us not to be rude, self-seeking, or easily angered. Genuine courtesy comes from the heart. It is far more than a feeling of social responsibility.

We all encounter rudeness and discourtesy. In many business places we are treated without much consideration. In some amusement parks we are rudely directed to stand in long lines, or roughly pushed out of the way. People may show a lack of consideration, and sometimes even rudeness, in some of our churches.

There is perhaps no place on earth where there is more potential for discourtesy than in the home. Yet here courtesy and consideration are most needed. Paul tells the Christians at Philippi to esteem others better than themselves (Phil. 2:3). While this applies to all Christian behavior in general, it is especially important for life in the Christian family. In all our relationships of love we are called to be filled with consideration, to treat each other fairly, and to live with understanding.

Courteous behavior has two requirements: first, "Love seeketh not its own. . . ." The unselfishness of true love becomes an important part of the Christian life. It has been said that when both husband and wife are seeking self, they do not have a marriage. One of the basic requirements of an intimate marriage is a deep desire to share with each other, to understand each other. This naturally leads to treating each other courteously, for this is love.

The second requirement for true courtesy is controlling one's temper: "Love . . . is not irritable or resentful." Have you ever watched drivers show their anger and impatience when the road is blocked by a stalled car or when someone does not go the instant the light turns green? Some people are not in the least embarrassed by such displays of temper: in fact, they pride themselves on their tempers. But a person who is easily provoked is not an easy person to live with.

Losing our temper is childish, and it is also contrary to the law of love. God loves us, and keeps on loving even when we are very unlovable.

His love is so great that He loved us when we were yet sinners. If we bear His image, profess to believe in Jesus, and want to be followers of God in the art of loving, there is little room for our childish and immature outbursts of temper—especially not in the home.

A boy who was invited to do something his parents would not condone said, "No, I can't do that. If I do, my dad will get awfully mad at me." If our children obey us because of our anger, what has happened to love? I would rather hear a boy say, "I wouldn't do that because it would hurt my dad, and I don't want to make him feel bad."

If we live in love, we will not want to hurt others. Our love for God will also grow. He first loved us—so we would not want to grieve Him by the things we do.

**Discussion Questions**

1. If people say, "I believe in telling it like it is," does this mean they are going to be perfectly honest or "perfectly" rude? Explain.

2. Some people can criticize us in a helpful way. Others tell us what they think and it hurts. What is the difference? Can we usually accept criticism from our mates rather well or does it bring resentment? Why do we react as we do?

3. Some people use a lot of crude language. Is this just a bad habit of speech or is it a lack of courtesy and good manners? How can we help our children develop good habits of speech?

Do you think they imitate us? How did your parents deal with your use of language?

4. Some church services are disrupted by rustling papers, shuffling feet, whispering, and other disturbing things. Does this show poor manners? Is it a lack of respect for the church and pastor? Or do people just feel that they should make themselves at home in church? Explain.

5. How do you react when you are waiting in line and someone else crowds in ahead of you? Should a Christian protest, or should he or she go the extra mile? Explain.

6. Do you think it is true that often we show less courtesy in the home and family than when we are around others? What causes this? Do you find it harder to show courtesy to a stranger whom you will never meet again, than to a friend? Why, or why not?

7. When someone gives a child some candy or a cookie, do you feel it is good for a parent to say, "Say thank-you to the man"? Is that a good way to teach a child good manners? Are there true Christians who lack courtesy?

# 9

# When Love and Evil Meet

## I Corinthians 13:6-7
## Matthew 7:1-5

It is quite evident that many people find delight in evil. They are fascinated by what television offers them: programs which feature infidelity, immorality, adultery, violence, and sadism. They willingly listen to the tragedies and violence of the day on the evening news—or read about it in their favorite newspaper or newsmagazine. People enjoy talking about and listening to others discuss evil occurrences. But such a fascination is contrary to the spirit of true love.

To the Christian all sin is sad. If a teen-ager in the congregation gets in trouble with the law, it brings deep sadness to his or her parents—not hatred, rejection, or hostility. Parents react this way because they love their child. They may not approve of the child's lifestyle, but they still love the child. God's love is like that too. He often hates the things we do, but He continues to love us.

Love hates evil. Love rejoices with the truth and with righteousness. We must always keep a sharp distinction between good and evil. Love does not take away that distinction. We must forgive the sinner in love, but we must not pretend that his or her sin is not evil. Love is tender and kind, but it stands firm against evil. We must all deal with the evil that surrounds us in the world. Even more basically we must all deal with the evil we find in our own lives and in the lives of our family members. No person is free from evil; no family can escape its power. We all must come to terms with its influence. How does a wife view the sinful acts or attitudes she sees in her husband? Does she laugh about them? Does she say that it only shows how human he is? Paul gives us four answers to this question in verse seven of this chapter on love.

First, love "bears all things." We do all we can to protect and help the person who sins. God has "covered" our sins in his love. We are to forgive, try to understand why, and do what we can to help.

Second, love "believes all things." Love takes the kindest view possible. It searches for the good and so tries to lift the sinner.

Third, love "hopes all things," for it seeks to build a new and better person, to reach towards newer heights. This is not just blind optimism, but confidence based on God's promises. A wife who was addicted to shoplifting came with her husband to the pastor to seek help. Since the problem had many psychological facets, she saw a Christian psychologist, and was helped to overcome her addiction.

Fourth, love also "endures all things," for we

do not reject the sinner. We continue to work and pray for them to conquer evil.

We often read of forest fires that devastate many acres of precious timberland. If you visit the area a year after the fire, however, you will notice many plants and small trees covering the blackened fields with green foliage. The healing love of a family is like that new foliage. When there is understanding between husbands and wives, parents and children, the evils and sins of life can bring out a stronger and more vibrant Christian character. Peter was a better man after he had denied his Lord and was restored by Christ. The prodigal was a better son after he came back from the far country. We need to help each other overcome the evils that still show their ugly heads from time to time. That is what marriage is—a relationship of love which promotes growth.

Love does not overplay the evils we see; it does not cover them up; it brings the kind of understanding that brings healing. In love we confess that none of us is perfect, that we all have a long way to go. But God's Word does give the assurance that God's love enables us to be more than conquerors. One of the most powerful ways of showing love is by accepting and caring for one who has fallen into sin. It isn't easy, for we are ready to condemn. But it is a strong urge in the heart of one who has felt the joy of God's forgiving love.

**Discussion Questions**

1. While riding home from a Bible class, one of the women said to the others, "Did you hear

the rumor about our pastor's sexual involvement with his secretary?" Why do we enjoy gossiping about someone who is caught in a public sin? Does it sometimes make us feel like we are better people when we talk about the sins of others?

2. What attitude should we take toward an unmarried girl who is pregnant? What attitude should parents take? Is it possible to be too loving and forgiving in reaction to others who condemn her harshly?

3. When a son commits a crime and is sent to prison, should parents ask for the public prayers of the church? How would you react if this happened in your family?

4. One night, after midnight, the police notified a father that his son had been caught using drugs. The father was asked to post bail, and then take his son home. How would you handle this situation if this were your son? Can we be too severe or too lenient when this happens?

5. Each of us faces temptations at work, in the community, and at home. What are some of the things you do to resist temptations? Why are some people more easily led astray than others?

6. Some people are honest only because it pays to be honest. Some keep themselves from sexual sins only because they are afraid they may get caught. Is that the way a Christian is to face life? If you could take money without any

danger of being caught, would you resist the temptation?

7. What does it mean to you that "love rejoices in the truth"? What does this teach us about the kind of love Paul extols in this chapter? Give examples of "rejoicing in the truth."

# 10

# Love Is Unconquerable
## I Corinthians 13:8-10

In this world nothing we see or touch is really permanent. We may talk about the everlasting mountains or the never-changing sea, but erosion slowly wears down the mountains and the shorelines of our seas are in a state of constant change. Paul was aware of the lack of permanence in life. In these verses Paul declares that while most things change, one thing is constant: love. Prophecies, speaking in tongues, knowledge—all these fade away. But love abides for it is eternal and unconquerable. It has its source in an everlasting, never-changing God.

There were some sharp conflicts in the church at Corinth. In his letter Paul deals with these disputes. Some members made a great deal of the gift of speaking in tongues; others were turned off by tongues-speaking. Some members emphasized the gift of prophecy; others disapproved of prophecy. Some claimed extraordinary spiritual knowledge; others rejected that claim. At the close of chapter 12 Paul promised to show the Corinthians a more excellent way—the way of love. The gifts of speaking, prophecy, and knowledge would fade away, but love remains constant.

The permanence of love is not a popular concept in our age. People easily fall in and out of love. They love someone one day; the next day they dislike that person. The easy acceptance of infidelity and divorce demonstrates that Christ's command to "love your neighbor as yourself" has not been taken seriously. This is a command, and it requires an act of the will. Love for our neighbor is not something we can choose to do or not to do.

It is well to stress once more the difference between *eros* love and *agape* love. Erotic love, the love that draws two people together in a passionate, physical way, is not very permanent. The beautiful face and the attractive form that seems so important in some marriages fades with the years—often more quickly than we would like. Erotic love is important, but it must always be a part of the true love, *agape*.

We marvel at the enduring power of the love of Christ. Peter denied Christ, but Christ seeks out Peter on that first Easter. Thomas with his doubts failed Christ, but Jesus lifts Thomas up again. The disciples failed Christ in the garden and at the cross, but all their failures did not dim Christ's love for them. We also fail Christ but His love does not waver. It is divine and eternal. Christ tells us, "Love one another, even as I have loved you."

The spirit of love within the church is often weak; sometimes it is hard to find. The members are supposed to be knit together as part of the family of God. We sing "all one body we" but often conflicts split the church into factions. One writer feels that this division is due to the fact that the church is often "worship centered" rather than "person centered." Churches may place much emphasis on "programs" while they are insensitive to the feelings and needs of the individual members. The quiet member, the one who is hurting, the one who feels left out—those people are easily, and often unintentionally, overlooked. This omission reminds us of the words of our Lord in Revelation 2:4, "You have left your first love."

God knows that we live in an imperfect world. The breakdown of family life brings tragic results. There is a variety of crime in our communities that breaks down the spirit of confidence and love. Nations are confused when one crisis follows another. But there is a reassuring note that runs through this hymn of love. We are promised that out of the imperfect shall one day come that which is perfect (v. 10). This guarantee lifts us to face the imperfection of today with the courage and hope that, by God's eternal love, we shall be victors in our spiritual battles. We are not to be satisfied with the imperfect, but we take comfort in the promise of future perfection.

Many things work against making love secure and permanent. More and more people get married with the thought that if things do not work out to their liking, the marriage can be dissolved. There is no real commitment to make the marriage permanent. Divorce is an easy way out, so many think today. If a marriage is to succeed, true and lasting love must rule the partners.

The permanence of our love can never measure up to the permanence of God's love for us, but we do find a pattern there. As God loves so ought we also to love. There is an unsurpassed beauty in a love that remains constant through all of life's experiences. To have a lifelong friend or a lifelong marriage can be one of life's greatest joys.

**Discussion Questions**

1. A husband or wife may become an alcoholic, be unfaithful, or "impossible to live with." How can a mate keep his or her love alive? Does our love change with changing circumstances?

2. Are there situations in a marriage when it is less of a sin to get a divorce than to continue living together? Some say that the real sin is not in the divorce itself, but in the things that lead to divorce. Do you agree? Why, or why not?

3. Is it possible for the love of parents to grow cold when a child is rebellious? How long must parents keep on loving a wayward son or daughter?

4. Can you describe your church as a "loving church"? How is love shown? What are some of the matters that interfere with love in the body of Christ? What can be done to create a more loving spirit?

5. We are told to "love our neighbors." Some communities are ruled by fear. The doors are doublebolted and people are afraid to go out

at night. How far should our love for neighbors go? Some people move out of depressed neighborhoods to the suburbs. Does that show love and concern for our neighbors?

6. There are many opposing forces at work in our world today: labor and management, the haves and the have–nots; racist and integrationist. How can love have an effect on such conflicting parties? Why would it sound strange to talk about love in a labor dispute?

7. Love helps couples grow. Is this a steady progress, or are there ups and downs? What are you doing to keep the spark of love alive in your marriage, or in your home? What help do we receive when we follow Christ as a pattern for our love (Eph. 5:24)?

# 11

## Growing into Mature Love

### I Corinthians 13:11
### II Peter 3:18

It's hard for us to imagine what Paul was like when he was a child. In fact, it's hard to imagine what many dignified people, such as the president or other national leaders, were like as children. It's even hard to picture ourselves as children, for we feel that we have been grown-up for so many years. Memories of the first few years of life are always vague.

In this passage Paul tells us that when he was a child, he spoke as a child, thought as a child, understood as a child. He had a lot of maturing to do. Paul compares the growing maturity of a child with spiritual growth from a babe in Christ to a mature believer. Even at his present level of spiritual maturity Paul knew he was a long way from the ultimate goal. As a child's imperfect speech and thinking matures into expression and understanding, so too, spiritually that which is still imperfect will be conquered by the final step of maturity—that of being with Christ and being like Him.

In some ways we all rebel against growing older and becoming more mature. We long for the carefree days of childhood when others made decisions for us and held our hands when we encountered distressful situations. Resist though we may, sooner or later we all reach the stage in life when we must lay aside our childish ways and seek to be mature in all our relationships.

The marks of maturity are hard to spell out. Some of the characteristics of maturity often mentioned are the ability to give as well as receive, the courage to be flexible, the endurance to live positively and constructively, and the grace to face the future—even death, without undue fear. Christians would also include the development of a seasoned faith. No one can ever list all of the factors that make a person mature because these factors will vary with the individual.

To mature also means that we outgrow our childish traits. This growth can be painful because it requires changes we often do not like to make. Some people manage to keep childish qualities throughout life, but this is not to their credit. Things such as temper tantrums, pouting to get our way, delight in childish pranks indicate that we have not really grown up.

Fritz Kunkel in his book *In Search of Maturity* writes that a child thinks in terms of "I" and "me." He is born an egoist. As we mature we learn to use the words *we* and *us* more often. We can gauge the level of maturity of a person by how often he or she uses the first-person pronoun.

But spiritual growth is more than getting rid of our childish habits. Growth requires not only subtraction but also addition. To overcome poor habits we must learn new habits to replace the old. Peter writes, "For this reason make every effort to supplement your faith with virtue, and virtue with knowledge, and knowledge with self-control, and self-control with steadfastness, and steadfastness with godliness, and godliness with brotherly affection, and brotherly affection with love" (II Peter 1:5-7).

So step by step we grow into mature, loving Christians. God provides all the help we need to build a life of love, to reach true nobility of character. There is grace sufficient so that we can face every trial and every disappointment as well as rejoice in every happy experience and through it all to come out "more than conquerors." But this growing requires a daily struggle, a constant climbing to reach new heights. We are not passive but active in the progressive growth of the love of God in Christ in our hearts and lives.

Life has a certain balance. When we lose something we gain something. The art of Christian love means that we exclude certain traits and qualities and we select newer and more satisfying qualities. Paul speaks of the things he "counted loss for the excellency of the knowledge of Christ Jesus, my Lord" (Phil. 3:8). We soon discover that the childish things we have outgrown are far outweighed by the spiritual gains we make.

The attainment of this spiritual goal is not by accident. We increase our physical strength by physical exercise; we increase our capacity to love by demonstrating love in specific actions. A deed of humility will make us more humble. Those who do nothing to help themselves grow will live stunted lives. Today it is so much easier to take flight than to stand firm and fight. We are reluctant to make difficult choices, hoping that by postponing action, the problem will vanish. We tend to find little joy in spiritual exercises, preferring to choose the easy road, the simple solution, and the comfortable pew. And so our spiritual lives are stunted. Growth demands daily exercise.

The real secret of growth is found in looking forward to the future. Our vision often is limited by the cares of today and the worries of tomorrow. We fail to see the distant scene. It is refreshing to know that the ultimate goal toward which we move is the grand climax of the maturing process in glory. When we see Him we shall be like Him. Then love will have reached its highest and noblest expression.

**Discussion Questions**

1. We describe some Christians as "babes in Christ." Is that a good term? Who are these people? How long may a person be considered to be a babe?

2. Some children are described as "little old men," or "little old ladies." What is meant by these expressions? How does a child get that way? Is this condition healthy for a child? Why, or why not? How will this affect a child as the years go on?

3. We sometimes describe a young person as being "mature for his years." Can we measure our maturity according to our age? Is it good for a person to be more mature than others of his age? Why, or why not?

4. Can a person who is emotionally immature be spiritually mature? Can a person who is spiritually immature be emotionally immature? Explain your answers.

5. We all know people whom we consider to have reached a high level of maturity. What are some of the qualities of such individuals?

6. On a scale of one to ten, ten being the highest level of maturity, where would you place yourself? Why do you give yourself that grade? How are you trying to reach a higher level?

7. In the Gospels Jesus condemns childishness (Matt. 11:9-19), but encourages childlikeness. What is the difference? What childlike qualities are listed in Matthew 18:1-6?

# 12

## The Perfection of Love

### I Corinthians 13:12
### I John 3:2

The mirrors used by the people of Corinth were made of polished brass or silver. The reflection they gave were at best distorted and blurred. Paul borrows this analogy to illustrate the imperfection of our vision in this life, for "we know in part." Now our spiritual vision does not reveal many of the details we would like to know, but then we shall see "face to face." Now we know only "in part," then we shall "know fully." We shall move from the imperfect to perfection, and our riddles and puzzles will be solved.

The vision we now have of God and of His world is glorious and comforting, even though there are many unanswered questions and enigmas. Moses, in a moment of high ecstasy, said to God, "I pray thee, show me thy glory." God wisely answered, "you cannot see my face; for man shall not see me and live." God then hid Moses in a cleft of the rock and allowed His glory to pass by while Moses was covered with God's hand. He was given a vision of God's back. That vision was exceedingly glorious, even though it did not show God's full glory (Exod. 33:18-23).

Our knowledge is wrapped in mystery. We see what God is doing and are often perplexed. We know He leads us, but we do not know where. We can know, love, trust, and worship Him, but we cannot comprehend Him. Jesus told His disciples that there were things He could not tell them because they would not be able to bear them. In His wisdom God withholds from us what the future will bring. The anticipation of future trials or future prosperity would rob us of the joy of the moment.

Our knowledge of man and the world are also limited. Men delve into the secrets of the universe, the forces of nature, the working of the body, and the mind of man, but soon reach the limits of science. The picture is blurred and distorted. The knowledge of the mysterious forces that make man and his world operate as it does includes many riddles we have not been able to solve. We know only in part for we see through a glass darkly. Our vision is imperfect.

The loftiest and most tangible revelation God gave of Himself was in the coming of His Son in human form. When we try to answer the question of a child, "What is God like?" our feeble faith can only point to the God-man. Jesus said, "He who has seen me has seen the Father" (John 14:9). That is a radiant glimpse of God. But our vision is still imperfect, for although we see God in the glass of His Word and feel His presence in our lives, we have yet to see Him "face to face." That is a vision we now are not able to bear, but when we look into His face "we shall know fully, even as we are known."

When we talk with a stranger by phone, or when we hear a person speak on the radio, we form a mental picture of the person. Often we are mistaken. When we meet the person face to face, we see a facial expression, a look in his eyes, a frown or a smile—someone who is quite different from our mental picture. A blind man, sightless from birth, had surgery that was to give him sight. He said that the first thing he would like to see was his mother's face. He had felt her gentle touch, heard her voice, but had never been able to see her.

It is good to know that someday our imperfect knowledge will be perfect, that the riddles of life will be solved, and we need no longer say, "I'm sorry, but I don't know." One day we will know the answers to all our questions. Every heart-break, every struggle, every penitential sigh, every shame and regret will be explained. We will also have a clear understanding of the joyful and prosperous experiences of life.

We will not be omniscient, only God has that attribute. We will have a knowledge that satisfies the deep longing of a person to know. The fondest longing for learning will be satisfied. A child goes through a stage in life when the question *why* is a daily concern. Whether we will admit it or not, we all ask that question too often. It is best for us that there is no answer here. Here we see the twisted knots and tangled threads of life's embroidery, there the beautiful pattern will be seen. Here we see the blueprints and plans of a building, there we see it a completed structure of beauty and usefulness.

We will also be known. We often feel alone and misunderstood. Even our loved ones fail to know our inner pain or our highest joy. Many people say, "no one understands, no one cares." In heaven our burden will be lifted for we will be known and understood by God and by others. Others will share with us in perfect vision, perfect knowledge, and perfect love.

The grand climax of love finds man once more restored into the image of God, redeemed from all sin and shame. John says, "we shall be like him, for we shall see him as he is." We will share in His glory, but also in His character. That is the grand climax of God's love. That is the end of the long journey out of the wanderings of sin in humble response to the Savior's call, "Come unto me."

Scripture encourages us to take the long view of life, to lift our eyes to the heights. We often focus only on the here and now. To live a full life we must gain the vision of the eternal perfection of love.

**Discussion Questions**

1. Why does God give us so little information about heaven and the life to come? Some say God wants us to live in the "now" and not in the future. Do you agree? Is there another reason?

2. There are a number of books on the subject of heaven. Some describe just what is going to take place there. The authors claim to have

made a special study of the subject. Are such books helpful to you? Is it true that such people know more about heaven than we do?

3. There have been a number of writings by people who claim to have been in heaven, and then returned. Could there be such a thing as coming back from death? How would you explain the accounts given by people who have been beyond death and returned again?

4. Have you ever thought or said, "I really don't care to go to heaven just yet. I rather enjoy life here"? Is it wrong to say that? Why, or why not? What does "heavenly-mindedness" mean to you?

5. A patient in severe pain repeatedly asked, "Why me, Lord?" The pastor who called on him said that it was sinful to ask that question. Do you agree with the pastor? Why, or why not? How would you reply to that patient?

6. What does the phrase, "take the long view of life" mean to you? Is that contrary to the words of Jesus in Matthew 6:34? How can the long view of life help in today's crises?

7. Our knowledge is only partial and imperfect. How does this apply to human relationships? Do you really know your husband or wife? Some scientists seem to know many things about, for example, the solar system, the human body, economics. Is their knowledge limited? Have we advanced further on the road to perfect knowledge than a previous generation or two? Is this scientific knowledge a gift of

God even when it is not used to His praise? Explain.

8. The world about us is marvelous and beautiful. Can you imagine what the "new earth" will be like? Why is our knowledge about the "new earth" so limited?

# 13

## The Superiority of Love

### I Corinthians 13:13
### Romans 13:8-10

Kierkegaard, the Danish writer, said that living in love is like paying off an infinite debt. It can never be paid in full. In fact, no matter how much we love, the debt is never reduced. Kierkegaard referred to our indebtedness to God's love—love in its pure form, eternal and unchanging. Our love is but a weak response to that infinite love, and as a result our "debt" is never reduced. But, according to Paul, love is still the greatest and most important thing in our lives.

With love, faith and hope also abide. In verse two Paul talks of the kind of faith that can move mountains. By faith he means that a person not only believes that God exists, but also has confidence and trust in God's character and in His relationship with us and the world. Faith is not a mere intellectual assent to a list of propositions, but rather a trusting response to God Himself. Faith needs the warmth of love to make it glow.

Hope is the anticipation of good to come. It is the power that urges human beings ever onward—in worthwhile endeavors, in patience and suffering, in high aspirations to reach the loftiest goals. People who have lost hope are inclined to say, "What's the use of striving to get ahead?" Others, even though living in poverty or fear, are able to say, "I know things will be better for my children." Hope is that strange power in a person that helps him or her to acquire that last bit of strength to reach a goal.

There are some very practical considerations that bind this beautiful chapter together in the context of the Christian family. I know, and I am sure you also know, families who seem to be firmly rooted in their faith. They are willing to defend their doctrines and traditions. They follow a regular routine of trying to live the life of faith—in worship, in prayer, and in fellowship—but there is a strange coldness about their spiritual life. They seem to lack the spirit of joy. They miss much of the real meaning of faith because they lack love. It is hard for the members of the family to say, "I love you," to each other, and to God.

But how do we learn to love? We learn to love as we share our joyful and painful moments with each other. We learn to love as we spend time with each other, whether that be a few years with children who leave when they are grown, or many years with a spouse. We learn to love as we live and travel together.

This is also true of the love we have for our Lord Jesus Christ. We stand on Bethlehem's hills and rejoice at the birth of the Christ child. We join with the crowds who listened to His message, His parables, and His teachings. We see His marvelous healing power. We hear the awesome groans of Gethsemane, watch with tears the events at Calvary, stand with joy and a sense of victory at the empty tomb in the garden. We see Him ascend to glory, and we live in the glad hope of His coming again. It is that abiding fellowship that teaches us to love Him. And out of that love flows a deep love for each other.

Today we find thousands of books that direct us to find our solutions to difficulties in better communication. Certainly this will help. But we must never, while loving each other, lose sight of the vertical aspect of love. Love within marriage is a love not only between two people, but a triangle of love, where the lines run not only between the marriage partners, but from each person to God.

This thirteenth chapter from Paul's first letter to the Corinthians tells us in unmistakable terms that love on a horizontal level may be *philos*, or even *eros*, but it can never be *agape*, the lofty love in which God has the central place. I have seen the power of that kind of love in many families. I can assure you that it works. There is a strange power in it which we can never define nor fully understand, but if we have surrendered to it, we know its power and reality.

In these brief studies we have tried to relate Paul's teachings to the family and to marriage. We are well aware that this touches only one facet of what he had in mind. Paul's teachings also relate to our neighbors, our enemies, and others throughout the world, for the world is truly starving for love.

**Discussion Questions**

1. Faith and hope are essential qualities for the Christian. Why does Paul consider love to be superior? Isn't it true that faith naturally leads to love?

2. Can two strong Christians clash? See Acts 15:35-41. Were Paul and Barnabas lacking in love? Was their solution an ideal one? Why, or why not?

3. Much that is written and sung about love today is rather cheap or sentimental. How does the love described in I Corinthians differ? Which qualities of love do we need more of today? What can we do to achieve these qualities?

4. "Sexual intimacy is the highest form of love between husband and wife," wrote an author on the subject of love as *eros*. How do you react to that comment? Is it possible to have *agape* even when there is no sexual intimacy? Explain. Can *eros* be a significant part of *agape*? If so, how?

5. Many conflicts arise in the family, the church, the community, industry, and education. Does this demonstrate a lack of love? Can there be conflict with love? Does a conflict between mates in marriage, or parents and children, show a lack of love?

6. There is a danger when we study a chapter a verse at a time that we lose some of its beauty.

Read again this whole hymn of love. What does this chapter say to you personally? How can you best practice the various truths presented?